SPORTS HEROES AND LEGENDS

Mia Hamm

Read all of the books in this exciting, action-packed biography series!

Hank Aaron

Barry Bonds

Joe DiMaggio

Tim Duncan

Dale Earnhardt Jr.

Lou Gehrig

Mia Hamm

Tony Hawk

Derek Jeter

Michael Jordan

Michelle Kwan

Mickey Mantle

Shaquille O'Neal

Jesse Owens

Jackie Robinson

Babe Ruth

Ichiro Suzuki

Tiger Woods

Mia Hamm

by Sean Adams

BARNES
& NOBLE

NEW YORK

For the Abels—

Ruthe, Marty, Barry, Sandy, Amy, and Melanie

Cover photograph:
© T. Mendoza/L.A. Daily News/CORBIS SYGMA

Barnes & Noble Publishing, Inc.
122 Fifth Avenue
New York, NY 10011

ISBN 0-7607-3469-0

Printed in the United States of America

05 06 07 08 MCH 11 10 9 8 7 6 5 4

Written by Liesa Abrams

Sports Heroes and Legends™ is a trademark of
Barnes & Noble Publishing, Inc.

Contents

Soccer's Sweetheart

Have there ever been so many people here?

It didn't seem possible to the members of the University of North Carolina women's soccer team as they stared around Fetzer Field on that sunny day in 1993. And they were right—close to 6,000 fans had packed the stands for the NCAA championship game between UNC and George Mason University, the largest crowd ever to attend a college women's soccer match.

The UNC women's soccer team had won the last straight seven championship games, and the U.S. women's team—made up of mostly UNC players—had won the first ever women's World Cup in 1991. But even with all the cool stuff they'd done, there usually weren't very many people at the team's games, even a championship match.

So why was this game so popular?

There was one reason why Fetzer Field was filled with fans

that day—the team's star player, Mia Hamm, was playing in her last college game.

Mia couldn't believe all those people were there just to see her play. She still didn't understand how she'd become so famous playing a sport that was barely noticed by most of the country.

Already, at just 21 years old, Mia had accomplished tons of amazing things on the field, helping her teammates to win after win—including the 1991 World Cup. Now she was playing in her final college game, and she didn't even know what to feel. As excited as she was to move on to new challenges, Mia couldn't help being a little sad about saying good-bye to the team she'd looked at as a second family.

But one thing was for sure—no way would Mia miss the chance to leave her mark one last time in a UNC championship game! Even though Mia's teammates had scored three goals in the first half, giving the UNC Tar Heels a comfortable lead, Mia entered the second half determined to find an opening and grab one last goal.

Of course, Mia could never do anything the easy way. Instead of waiting to make a play while her team was on offense, Mia ran in for a steal and kicked the ball away from a George Mason player, redirecting it back down to the other end of the field. As always, she easily dodged defenders and zoomed across the grass, showing off her incredible speed. At just the right moment she launched the ball toward the goal. The George Mason goaltender made a valiant effort, but the ball slammed past her and into the net.

Score!

The crowd roared for Mia, but all she cared about was that she was giving her team one more stellar effort before leaving. Once UNC's win was guaranteed, Mia's coach pulled her from the game to rest. Mia was surprised and overwhelmed to face a standing ovation from the fans as she jogged back to the bench. It was a little much for her, and she still was shy in the face of all that attention.

But it felt great to see those thousands of people cheering for a women's soccer game. For as far back as Mia could remember, all she'd wanted was for women's soccer to become as huge in America as the more popular sports, like baseball or basketball. As Mia thanked the fans for their support, she started to imagine what would come next for her. She knew one thing for sure—if she had anything to say about it, even bigger crowds would soon be coming to watch her play the sport she loved more than anything in the world.

Chapter One

Beating the Boys

Mia knew firsthand how little attention America paid to soccer. After all, it had taken living in another country to inspire *her* love of the sport, and she sometimes wondered how different things would have been if she'd grown up in the United States.

Mia was born in Selma, Alabama, on March 17, 1972, but her father, William Hamm, was a pilot in the U.S. Air Force and often had to move around for his job. Mia was barely a year old when Bill had to pick up and move himself, his wife, Stephanie, Mia, and Mia's two older brothers and two older sisters to Florence, Italy.

Bill was a huge sports fan, but he soon learned that the sports he'd watched back home—football, baseball, and basketball—weren't as popular in Italy. Instead Italians were hooked on soccer, a sport that fell pretty far under the radar in America.

At the time very few public schools and colleges in the United States had soccer teams, and barely anyone went to any of the North American Soccer League's professional games, which were rarely shown on TV.

But Bill realized that if he and his family wanted to keep watching sports, they'd have to learn more about the rules of soccer so they could start following the games. And once Bill understood the roles of the different players and how the game worked, he saw why soccer was so popular in Europe and South America. The scores were much lower than typical scores in a game like basketball, but that was part of what made soccer exciting—the constant pressure on a team to score a goal when scoring was so tough and the incredible thrill that came when someone *did* score.

❝*I have the best parents in the world. They encouraged me, but never pushed.*❞

—MIA HAMM

The entire Hamm family became huge soccer fans, so Mia spent her toddler years in Italy watching soccer matches on television and even joining her siblings in the backyard to kick the ball around.

By the time Bill was sent back to America, the love for soccer was in Mia's blood, and even though she was still only a few years old, she was anxious to play whenever she could.

The Hamms spent a short time in California and then moved to Wichita Falls, Texas, where they'd remain until Mia was in high school. At first Mia's parents worried that their children would have trouble finding other kids to play soccer with since the sport was so much less popular in their home country. But they were thrilled to find out that there was actually a youth soccer program in Wichita Falls. Mia's older siblings joined, but Mia was still too young and had to settle for watching the games from the sidelines. She would eagerly chase after the ball anytime it got kicked out-of-bounds, but that just wasn't enough for her.

When Mia turned five, her mother decided to send her to a ballet class, hoping that the combination of Mia's small build and boundless energy would make her a natural ballerina. Stephanie Hamm had loved ballet as a girl and had believed since Mia was an infant that her youngest daughter would follow in her footsteps. In fact, the name on Mia's birth certificate is actually Mariel Margaret Hamm, but her mother nicknamed her Mia as a baby because she reminded her so much of a former ballet teacher named Mia!

But Mia's mom was in for some disappointment—it took Mia only one class to decide that ballet was *not* for her. "I hated it," Mia admitted later. Even at five, Mia already knew exactly where she wanted to be, and it wasn't in a ballet studio—it was out on the field, playing soccer.

66For as far back as I can remember, I played [soccer] all the time at recess in grade school. . . . I came home with skinned knees on more than one occasion because I was going to do everything I could to beat the boys.99

—MIA HAMM

Finally she got her wish. Her parents signed her up for an organized team, trying not to worry about how much younger and smaller she was than most of the other players. There was just no keeping Mia away from soccer any longer!

Soon Mia proved that she had the natural abilities to match her excitement. "Our team record wasn't very good," she later remembered, "but I did manage to score a lot of goals."

When Mia's parents adopted a Thai American orphan in 1977, eight-year-old Garrett, Mia was handed the perfect play-mate. Her siblings enjoyed sports, but they had other hobbies, too. Garrett was as passionate about sports as Mia was, and the two of them spent endless hours playing together. Sometimes they played in pickup games with other neighborhood kids, and it didn't take long before they realized they could get away with something. Because Mia could fool the older boys into thinking she wasn't much of a threat, Garrett started calling her his "secret weapon."

"No one else would pick me because I was this quiet little girl," Mia shares. "Boy, did they regret it."

Garrett would always make sure that Mia was on his team, and she would help him put the opposition away.

Mia's talents didn't stay secret for long, and as she got older, she joined as many teams as she could. She was one of the first girls in Wichita Falls to play Little League baseball, shocking the all-boy teams with her speed and skills. In seventh grade she even joined her junior high school's *football* team. The boys on the team had no problem with that—in fact, they were the ones who convinced the coach to bring her on board! They knew Mia was as good—if not better—than they at the rough, physical game. Still, as amazing as Mia was at every sport she tried, it became hard to stay competitive in

At age 14 Mia joined a scrimmage—in the rain—with a team made up of all 16-year-old boys. She went on to score all three goals in the game, giving her team a 3–0 victory!

sports like football or basketball as she got older, because she was so small.

Luckily that was okay with Mia since just one sport came first for her, as it always had—soccer. And being small isn't a problem in soccer. Her size was even helpful in some ways because she could more easily dodge defenders and take off for a lightning-speed sprint down the field.

In 1982 Mia and her family couldn't wait to tune in to the World Cup games. They were frustrated to find out that the matches wouldn't be televised on American television, but since they lived in Texas, they were able to get the signal from Mexico, where the World Cup was a huge deal. The entire Hamm family was glued to the TV for every game, down to the final match between Italy and West Germany, where they were psyched to see Italy snag the medal after defeating their opponents 3–1.

But to Mia, the event was more than just something exciting to watch. She ached to be out there herself someday, competing in (and winning!) a World Cup tournament. But how would she manage that when she lived in a country where soccer was barely noticed? The U.S. team hadn't even qualified for the final World Cup round since 1950. Besides, there weren't any women in the World Cup from *any* country. As impossible as her dream seemed at the time, Mia promised herself that she'd find a way to make it happen.

It was almost like someone out there heard Mia's wish. That same year the NCAA began the first national college tournament in soccer, and the United States also put together its first women's soccer team for international competition. The buzz began that maybe men's and women's soccer would become medal events in the Olympics sometime soon and also that a women's World Cup tournament could become a reality. The stage was being set for Mia to one day see her dreams come true. All she had to do was make sure she was ready when the time came!

That didn't seem like it would be a problem. Mia was getting better and better all the time, and Lou Pearce, a local high school coach who watched Mia in many of her matches, felt that her experience playing with boys was a major factor. "By working with the boys all the time, she developed skills beyond her years and at a higher level than the other girls," Pearce explains. Looking back, Mia's pretty sure that Pearce is right but points out another way that joining boys' teams helped her. "Playing with boys reinforced my will to win and instilled a kind of fearlessness at any age," she says.

It didn't hurt that Mia continued to be the star of every boys' team she played on. Her last game with a youth league was the under-14 city championship, when she was 13. Surrounded by an all-male team, Mia dazzled on defense, keeping the opposing team's leading scorer from getting a goal. On the other end of the field she slammed in the game-tying shot that eventually allowed her Wichita Falls team to win the title in an overtime penalty kick shoot-out.

"*The other players were predictable, but Mia flowed. She was beyond her years in what she was doing.*"
—Wichita Falls high school coach Lou Pearce,
describing Mia's performance while she was
still in elementary school

Heads were starting to turn, and that year Mia was named a Texas All-State player in women's soccer. Mia was psyched about the award, but mostly because it meant that now she could play in some bigger tournaments and all-star games across the state, joining other players who loved soccer as much as she did.

It was at one of these games that Mia was spotted by John Cossaboon. Cossaboon was coach of the recently born U.S. women's soccer Olympic development team. He was always scouting the 16- and 17-year-old players so he could recommend the best ones to college coaches. He hoped the coaches would take the players' raw talents and shape them into professional-quality athletes—ready to join Cossaboon's squad. But when Cossaboon saw 14-year-old Mia Hamm, he did a double take.

How was it that he had never heard of this girl before? She was amazing! He watched with his jaw hanging open as Mia whizzed around the field, winging perfect passes to her teammates and moving toward the goal with obvious hunger and fire. He'd never seen anything like it. She was the smallest player on the field, but her determination, stamina, strength, and speed were absolutely unmatched.

Cossaboon didn't think he could be any more impressed, but then he found out how old Mia was. She was not only the smallest but also the youngest player out there and had still blown him away. This girl was definitely something special.

After the game Cossaboon stunned Mia and her parents by telling them that even at 14—just starting high school—Mia was just as good as college players. Until she was old enough to go away to school, he wanted her to join his Olympic development squad so he could start training her to be the soccer superstar he knew she would be one day.

Mia was totally ecstatic. For the first time it looked like a career playing soccer was really possible for her. It was all she'd ever wanted. Now she just had to prove she was up to the challenge.

Chapter | Two

Secret Weapon

Mia wanted more than anything to believe that John Cossaboon was right about her, but she was scared to get her hopes up. What if other coaches out there didn't agree with him?

Cossaboon also wanted someone to back him up, so he gave his friend and fellow women's soccer coach Anson Dorrance a call. Dorrance was probably the most famous coach in college soccer at the time. He headed up both the men's squad and the women's squad at University of North Carolina, where he'd once been a student and player himself, and also coached the U.S. women's national team. He'd guided his 1982 UNC team to a win at the first ever NCAA women's soccer championship, and the team had continued to dominate the championships over the years since. There was no question that Dorrance knew a talented women's soccer player when he saw one. So what would he think of Mia?

When Dorrance agreed to come and check Mia out at an under-19 national tournament in New Orleans, Louisiana, he had one condition—he didn't want Cossaboon to point her out. The true test would be if Dorrance could spot all on his own the player Cossaboon had raved about.

It took Dorrance less than a minute to pick her out. She was *that* good. "I watched her take a seven-yard run at the ball," he later explained, "and I said, 'Oh, my gosh!' I'd never seen speed like that in the women's game."

❝*I see this skinny brunette take off like she had been shot out of a cannon.***❞**

—ANSON DORRANCE, ON HIS FIRST "MIA SIGHTING"

Dorrance invited Mia to come to an upcoming training camp for his national team, where she'd have a chance to try out for a position on the squad. Dorrance wasn't worried about the fact that Mia was only 15 years old and the youngest women on the squad were already in college. He knew she could handle it. Mia wasn't so sure—it was pretty intimidating—but there was no way she could turn down an offer like that. She'd be there!

Mia showed up for her first day of training camp bursting with excitement. She couldn't wait to get out there on the field and let loose, and she still couldn't believe she'd actually be getting to practice with players she looked up to so much, like powerful striker Michelle Akers.

But Mia was in for a harsh wake-up call. Practice with the squad was tougher than anything she'd ever experienced. Before the team even stepped foot on the field, they had to spend hours indoors working out with weights and other exercise equipment. Mia had never lifted weights or spent much time in a gym. Why bother when she could be outside playing soccer instead? So even though she was a fit athlete, she suddenly had to use her muscles in a way she wasn't used to, and by the end her body felt bruised and battered. *Then* it was time to sprint outside and run through soccer drills and scrimmages. All Mia could think was—wait a second, there's more? "When I first did fitness with the national team, I thought I'd die," she admitted later.

But Mia made it through the day, and as wiped out as she felt that night, she knew deep inside that she was exactly where she belonged. "I loved how competitive [the national team] was," she says. "I was like, 'Wow. Look how hard these players work.'" Mia had played with *boys* who fought that hard to win before but never girls. Now for the first time Mia was surrounded by women players who shared her passion for soccer and were just as determined to come out on top. Her only worry was whether she could fit in. "Back then . . . I was shy and a bit intimidated by players I had idolized," she recalls. "But each day I attempted to play up to their level and earn their respect."

Mia put all her energy into building stamina and muscle and also into learning more about the strategy of soccer. She had natural speed and ability, but she was used to doing what came easily instead of learning how to work within a team of people who all had individual strengths and weaknesses. "I realized I was way behind the veteran players technically, tactically, and mentally," she explains. That was where Anson Dorrance came in. He worked hard to teach Mia how to transform herself from simply a good player into a good and *smart* player.

---

66 *For this shy kid, sports was an easy way to make friends and express myself.* 99

—MIA HAMM

Mia returned home at the end of training physically exhausted but mentally more keyed up about soccer than ever before. "She came back from camp and said she wanted to do two things," Mia's father later shared. "Go to North Carolina [for college], and win the world championship."

Pretty big dreams, huh? Well, if anyone could do it, Bill Hamm knew his daughter would!

The first sign that Mia was headed in the right direction came the summer of 1987, when she was officially named to Dorrance's women's U.S. national team. She was going to play in her first international competition! It was time to pack her bags and travel all the way to China for two games against the Chinese national team.

The first game took place on August 3, in the Chinese city of Tianjin. Since Mia was still a junior member of the team, she was a substitute—coming in off the bench to allow one of the starting players to rest. But even though she was only playing for a small amount of the game, those moments meant everything to Mia. This was her big chance. She knew she probably wouldn't do anything amazing like score a goal. She just hoped she wouldn't do anything *wrong* and hurt her teammates.

As if that could happen!

Mia kept her nerves in check, trying not to think about the thousands of fans watching—more people than she'd ever played for in her life. Coach Dorrance had been working with her to improve her defense since so far she'd really concentrated on scoring. This time she made sure to do what he advised and just focus on not letting the ball get in the hands (well, feet, actually!) of the Chinese players. She made every second she played count and was relieved to walk off the field without making a single mistake. Even better, the U.S. team won the game, 2–0!

I am a member of a team, and I rely on the team, I defer to it and sacrifice for it, because the team, not the individual, is the ultimate champion.

—MIA HAMM

Mia was floating on air when she got back home, full of exciting stories to share with her family. And the excitement was only beginning. Later that year Mia got special permission to take her December break from school early so she could rejoin the national team for a tournament of games taking place in Taiwan. She had a great time but worried that she wasn't catching on fast enough. "There were times I played for the national team when I felt like I was always in the wrong place," she remembers. "I never knew where to run, why to run, or how to run."

She may have felt like she wasn't keeping up, but Coach Dorrance sure didn't agree. After her performance in one of the games in Taiwan, he pulled her aside and told her, "Mia, you can become the best soccer player in the world." He couldn't wait to get her on his team at UNC.

Mia was just as excited to start playing college soccer, but before she could get there, she still had to finish high school. And it looked like that wouldn't happen in Texas because Bill Hamm got another transfer before Mia's junior year—the family had to move to Burke, Virginia.

Mia was a little sad about leaving Wichita Falls, which had been her home for longer than anywhere else she'd lived. But she was used to moving, and she knew she'd be able to meet new people, thanks to her favorite sport. "Soccer was a way to hang out and make friends," she says. "You move and have new friends as soon as you join a team." The added bonus of living in northern Virginia was that she'd be closer to the friends she'd already made on the UNC Tar Heels team—and to the university itself, where she was itching to be.

Mia got more good news after starting classes at Lake Braddock High School that fall. First, her parents and the school agreed to let her double up her course load so she could graduate a year early, meaning UNC was only one year away. And second, Mia learned that girls' soccer was actually a big deal in the Virginia suburbs around Washington, D.C. In fact, the Lake Braddock Bruins had made it to the state championship the past two years in a row.

Mia didn't mind that they hadn't actually won the previous year because now she had a mission—to help her teammates regain their title.

Since soccer was a spring sport, Mia joined a local club team that fall, the Braddock Road Shooting Stars, so she could stay in shape and keep working on her skills. By the time the Bruins' season began that spring, Mia was ready—and her teammates were ready *for* her after everything they'd already seen her do.

Mia didn't let anyone down. Her coach, Coach Rice, played Mia as forward along with two talented and experienced members of the team, Collette Cunningham and Liz Pike. Coach Rice was worried at first that Collette and Liz might be upset to be overshadowed by the team's new star, but it didn't take long for everyone to see that Mia's abilities came along with a very shy, humble nature. She wasn't a selfish player, on the field or off. All she wanted was to find a way to work with her team and help make everyone better. "The thing that stands out about Mia," Coach Rice told a reporter, "is her attention to the details of every task. She works hard to push herself, but by her own actions, she also motivates and encourages the others to work even harder."

Together the Bruins barreled through their season, knocking out every opponent who tried to challenge them. But as the postseason approached, the team lost two games, to Woodson and West Springfield. Suddenly the championship wasn't such a sure thing. But Mia and her teammates rallied themselves to stay strong and come back fighting. They went on to take the rest of their games and qualified for the state tournament. Now all they had to do was win it!

Mia was determined to contribute, and her two goals in the semifinal match against Monocan helped the Bruins to their 5–1 victory. Now it was on to the finals, where they would face their archrival, Woodbridge High. The Bruins couldn't have been happier. It was Woodbridge who had stolen the championship from them last year, so winning this time around would be a double victory.

Mia, Collette Cunningham, and Liz Pike turned in two goals each to help the Braddock Road Shooting Stars destroy Canada, with a final score of 8–0, in the club team's tournament—held the day after Braddock High's championship win!

Fourteen minutes into the game the score was still 0–0. Mia was being covered by Susan Braun, Woodbridge's best defender, who was sticking to her like glue. But the second Mia saw one of her teammates make a steal, she zoomed away from Braun and headed straight for the Woodbridge goal. After perfectly trapping the ball from her teammate's pass, Mia dribbled forward, faking out the defender who rushed out to challenge her. Now all that stood between Mia and a Bruins goal was Woodbridge's goaltender, Erin Tierney. Mia knew Tierney was good, but as she whammed the ball hard from right outside the penalty box, she hoped that *she* was better.

Tierney leapt into the air, reaching out to grab the ball, but it sailed past her into the right-hand corner of the net. Mia had scored the first goal of the championship game!

One goal was never enough for Mia, so she struggled to free herself of Braun and the other defenders who swarmed around her whenever she got close to the ball. Eventually she managed to break away and make a clean assist to Collette Cunningham, bringing the score to 2–0. One more goal from Mia and another from her teammate brought the Bruins to a total of four goals, which gave them a 4–1 victory. Lake Braddock had their championship title back, thanks to Mia!

Mia had a great time playing with the Bruins and was psyched to be part of their championship win. But as soon as the season ended, she was already moving on. She sure had a lot waiting for her—first another summer with the national squad and then, in the fall, starting college at UNC!

Chapter Three

Team Player

Most college freshmen feel pretty nervous when they start school because they're in a totally different place and meeting all new people. But Mia had it easy when she arrived at the University of North Carolina in the fall of 1989—thanks to soccer, she already had tons of close friends there!

Not only was Mia psyched to be with the friends she'd made on the U.S. national team, like her best friend and fellow freshman Kristine Lilly, but she also had coach Anson Dorrance there to look out for her. Dorrance had become much more than a trusted coach to Mia—he was more like a second father. He even became her legal guardian when her parents moved back to Italy for Bill's job. "[Anson Dorrance] was the driving force behind my growth as a person and a player," Mia shared. "He taught me that it was okay to want to be the best and pushed me toward that goal."

Mia was more determined than ever to sharpen her skills

on the soccer field now that she was playing for such an awe-some team. The UNC Tar Heels hadn't been beaten since 1985 and had held on to the NCAA championship title for the past three years running. Mia was dying to help them get a fourth straight title, but she also knew that she was a freshman on a team packed with talent, including two-time NCAA Player of the Year Shannon Higgins. For the first time in her life Mia would be playing on a team where she wasn't the star. So just how big a role would Mia have in the Tar Heels games?

A giant one, if Mia had anything to say about it!

Shannon continued to dominate on the field from her posi-tion as midfielder, leading the team and proving she deserved all her awards. But Mia and Kristine Lilly, both playing forward, were right there with her. The two freshmen were incredible on offense, their rhythm together adding a spark to the team that seemed almost like magic. Dorrance even called that year's group "the most exciting team we've ever had."

---

66 *Carolina is my home. I grew tremendously as a person and player in Chapel Hill, and if it wasn't for my Carolina experience, I definitely wouldn't be where I am today.* 99

—MIA HAMM

The magic worked, and the Tar Heels finished the regular season undefeated once again. Of their 22 games, only one was a tie. UNC grabbed the top scores at each of the other 21 matches, ending the season with a 12-game winning streak. For Mia it was a chance to learn how to work within a group and share the responsibility with players whose skills were equal to her own. And even though it was a new experience, she loved it—being a true team player was what she'd always wanted.

Now that the team had dominated another regular season, it was time for the Atlantic Coast Conference (ACC) tournament, where UNC would face the North Carolina State Wolfpack. Mia knew her older teammates had extra motivation to take the Wolfpack down. Last year, even though UNC had won the national championship, they had actually tied with NC State for the ACC championship. The title was decided by penalty kicks, where each team has the chance to take direct shots on the goalkeeper. NC State won the tiebreaker, making them the official champions even though UNC technically hadn't been defeated. The Tar Heels were ready for revenge—they wanted that ACC championship title back!

From the outside, it looked like an easy bet. The seemingly unbeatable UNC squad was playing a team with a much weaker record of only 13 wins, seven losses, and two ties. The Tar Heels weren't expecting much of a fight, so they let their guard down a little. They realized their mistake fast after their normally tough defense let in a whopping three goals, giving NC State an unexpected edge. The UNC players started to get scared—not only were they facing a repeat of last year, losing the ACC title again, but if things kept going like this, they would also see their undefeated streak come to an end right here, right now. Someone had to take action, and fast.

Not many people know it, but along with soccer Mia also played another sport at UNC—intramural basketball. Inspired by fellow Tar Heel Michael Jordan (one of Mia's favorite athletes and personal heroes), she was a real threat on the court, even at just five-foot four!

Well, guess who stepped up to the plate? Mia, of course! Mia and Kristine Lilly came through for their teammates big time, turning up the offensive juice and fighting back hard. Amazingly, the two freshmen poured in two goals *each*. Their hard work helped the Tar Heels to a 5–3 triumph over NC State, returning the ACC championship title to UNC. Mia was thrilled to be such a huge part of the victory, and her efforts were singled out when she was awarded the MVP trophy for the tournament. At the start of the season she'd only hoped to be able to *contribute* to UNC's success. Now here she was, leading the charge!

But the battle wasn't over yet. Now UNC had to defend their NCAA title. And after crushing Hartford with a 9–0 win in the quarterfinals, UNC was up against a familiar enemy for the chance to move on to the finals—the NC State Wolfpack, who had also qualified for the NCAA tournament.

Mia and her partner in crime, Kristine Lilly, weren't about to let the Wolfpack get away with anything. Mia, always on the lookout for her chance, grabbed a loose ball in the first half and nailed it into the goal to give the Tar Heels a one-point lead. Meanwhile UNC's defense played their opponents hard, determined not to let any goals get by this time. Then Kristine matched Mia's goal with one of her own early in the second half. The rest of the match was scoreless, making Mia's and Kristine's shots the only goals of the day—and the winning ones!

Thanks to the powerhouse team of Mia and Kristine Lilly, the Tar Heels were moving on to the NCAA finals against Connecticut. In the all-important championship game the two "superfrosh" left the scoring to their teammates but turned in their usual top-notch performances to help UNC hold on to the edge. Player of the Year Shannon Higgins made the second—and game-winning—goal for UNC, giving the team a final score of 2–0. Mia was ecstatic. In her first year at UNC she'd become an NCAA champion!

Not only that, but Mia had an extra bonus. Even though Higgins and Kristine Lilly had gotten more attention for their playing that year, when all the stats were added up, it was Mia who took the top spot for scoring. Mia, a freshman *and* the youngest player on the team, had made an amazing 21 of the team's goals that season.

Still, even though the year seemed like a perfect success, Mia wasn't satisfied with herself. She knew she was a strong scoring option, but she wanted to be a more well-rounded player, like Higgins. The athletes she most admired were the ones who could be counted on for powerful offense *and* tight defense, and she wouldn't be happy until her teammates could feel that way about her.

Mia spent the summer working hard on improving the other areas of her game. She drilled Coach Dorrance nonstop for advice on what her weaknesses were and how she could improve her skills, spending endless hours practicing her technique.

But the summer wasn't all work and no play. Mia traveled with the national team to take on some tough opponents, beginning with Norway, one of the best women's soccer teams in the world. Norway's excellent reputation made the moment that much sweeter when Mia knocked in her first goal of international competition during the match. Mia was just warming up, and she went on to score four goals in the five games she played in with the national team that summer. Team USA had their most successful season yet, winning all six of their games (Mia missed just one), and Mia had been there to help make it happen!

Now that Mia had made her mark on the national team *and* worked with Coach Dorrance to become more of a complete player, she was definitely ready to jump back into the action at UNC in the fall. And she knew the team needed her more than ever, now that Shannon Higgins had graduated, leaving one of the youngest teams since the UNC women's soccer program had begun in 1979. It was time for Mia to find out if she was up to the challenge of taking a leader's position on the squad.

The answer came sooner than anyone expected. On September 22 the Tar Heels traveled to Connecticut to face the UConn Huskies. The Huskies played UNC hard, and for once the Tar Heels found themselves struggling to hold off an opponent. Many of the UNC players were nervous about whether the team was as strong as it had been in the past. The tough UConn team took advantage of this, doing their best to intimidate them. Only Mia kept her focus, scoring both of UNC's goals and pushing the game into overtime. But when the final seconds came, UConn's lead of 3–2 made them the winner. Stunned and heartbroken, the Tar Heels had to face the end of their incredibly long undefeated streak. The number stood at a whopping 103 games, but it still wasn't enough for Mia and her teammates. Even though they knew deep down it wasn't true, they couldn't help feeling like they had let down Higgins and the other star players who'd come before them at UNC.

If the team was shaky before that game, they were a wreck afterward, their confidence totally blown to pieces. A week later they were up against George Mason University. UNC had George Mason beat on pure talent, but they were so thrown by the previous week's loss that they weren't playing with enough fire and determination. They were doubting themselves, and it showed.

Mia knew that if she didn't do something, the Tar Heels were headed for trouble. So she fought back her own doubts and forced herself to remember that she could do it—she could win this game. Even after the George Mason goaltender made save after save, Mia never gave up hope. The scoreless game was down to just *15 seconds* left, and Mia was still totally alert and ready for her chance.

And finally she found it. In fact, she *made* it happen when she forced a George Mason defender into making a bad pass that she quickly intercepted. Immediately Mia took off down the field with the ball, racing toward the goal. Knowing she had only one chance to get this right, Mia faked out the George Mason goaltender and put her whole body into a kick that sent the ball sailing into the net. There were eight seconds left in the game, and Mia's goal gave the Tar Heels the win. More importantly, the thrilling play jump-started their confidence, and it wasn't long before UNC was back on top, dominating their conference.

Coach Dorrance was especially impressed by the four goals Mia made with the national team in the summer of 1990 because she made them coming into games as a substitute. Of the 450 possible minutes of playing time, Mia was on the field for a total of only 270 minutes—and she *still* made such a high number of goals!

By the time the ACC tournament rolled around, many of Mia's teammates had stepped up and had strong seasons, but they still counted on Mia in crunch time. And she showed everyone why in the ACC finals, when her one goal and one assist gave UNC the win over their opponents, the Virginia Cavaliers.

With the ACC title under their belt, the Tar Heels moved on to the NCAA championship. They couldn't have been more

Mia's UNC soccer jersey, number 19, was retired after she graduated, in a special ceremony during halftime of a UNC basketball game against Duke in 1994. Mia was one of several former Tar Heels whose numbers were retired that night, along with her friend Kristine Lilly and Michael Jordan!

excited about the team they were facing—the UConn Huskies. This was their chance to get back what the Huskies had stolen in September. But as much as they wanted the chance to destroy UConn, Mia and her teammates couldn't help wondering—were they up to the challenge?

Chapter Four

Trailblazer

As Mia and the rest of the Tar Heel squad got ready for the NCAA finals game against Connecticut, they told themselves that all they needed to do was keep their confidence up. They knew their bodies were ready to win this game—now they just had to make sure their minds were, too. "Coach told us to remember who we are and what it means to play for North Carolina," Mia later explained. "We wanted to bury them psychologically in the first fifteen minutes."

Showing what a strong team they'd become, Mia and her teammates followed Coach Dorrance's advice and played their hearts out. The UConn defense kept a stranglehold on Mia but soon discovered that she wasn't the only threat on the field. Mia was actually acting as a decoy on purpose to open up the field for the rest of the offense. Kristine Lilly scored two goals in the first half, and UNC got off more than three times as many shots as the Huskies. Things only got worse for UConn in the second half, as UNC's tight defense limited UConn to only three shots—none of which they made—while the Tar Heels offense knocked in another four goals. The final 6–0 triumph was sweeter than any of the wins UNC had enjoyed in a long time, and it gave them their fifth straight NCAA championship title.

> **❝** *I always make sure I thank or hug the person who gave me an assist on a goal because the point belongs to her as much as to me.* **❞**
>
> —MIA HAMM

It had been an incredible season for Mia, coming back from a crushing loss to lead her team to ultimate victory. This year she was not only the top scorer for her team but also for the entire NCAA, with 24 goals and 19 assists. But as exciting as the past months had been, Mia knew it was nothing compared to what she was about to experience. She was going to play in the first women's World Cup ever!

Back when Mia was a little girl, she'd dreamed of playing in the World Cup even when everyone told her it would never be possible. Over the summer of 1990 her wish had been granted. The international soccer association, FIFA, had announced they were going to sponsor the first women's World Cup in 1991. Mia knew she had to be right there playing for Team USA, even though it meant some hefty sacrifices.

Since competitive women's soccer was still pretty new in America, the players would need to dedicate themselves entirely to training if they hoped to have a chance against the experienced and tough teams they'd face at the World Cup. That meant no time for school or jobs or even for family. Mia would have to leave UNC so she could join the rest of the national team in early January 1991 to start practicing for long hours every single day and then spend the spring and summer in international matches and qualifying events for the World Cup.

As hard as it was for Mia to take time away from college, she knew some of her teammates were giving up even more than she was, and none of them was getting much in return. While members of the men's national team were paid a salary, the women were only given free housing and food, with no extra benefits. But Mia didn't see it like that—if her only payment was being able to play in a World Cup, that was enough for her!

This time, though, Mia's pure dedication and scoring power wouldn't be enough to guarantee her a spot on the World Cup team. Coach Dorrance was making everyone try out for their positions, pushing the women to play to their top potential. Mia rose to the challenge, as Dorrance knew she would, and was named a reserve forward. That meant she would substitute for one of the three starting offensive players—the national team's captain, April Heinrichs, dynamo striker Michelle Akers, and Mia's personal hero Carin Gabarra.

Mia was perfectly happy to come in off the bench, but after an unexpected twist she ended up in the starting lineup herself! Unfortunately, one of the starting defenders suffered a bad knee injury before the women's World Cup tournament began. To Mia's surprise, Coach Dorrance asked her to switch from playing backup forward to starting right midfielder, a position with intense defensive responsibilities as well as a role in scoring. It would definitely be a challenge, and Mia was a little scared. "I just didn't want to make a mistake," she admitted. But at the same time she realized this was what she really needed. Now she'd *have* to develop her abilities on defense to the same level as her offensive skills, something she was still working on.

Even with all the changes, the national team's grueling winter practice schedule paid off in their early spring games. Their first tournament took place in Bulgaria, where they won matches against Hungary, France, Yugoslavia, and the USSR, keeping these opponents from scoring even one goal. Next it was on to Haiti for a round-robin tournament where Team USA again dominated, easily winning all five games and racking up an incredible 47 goals total.

But the U.S. squad faced stiffer competition from the European teams they battled next, winning just three out of five games against France, England, Holland, Denmark, and Germany. These matches were called "friendlies" because the results didn't actually count, but it was still a warning to the U.S. team that they needed to shape up before the real deal in the fall.

 At 19, Mia was the youngest member of the 1991 U.S. World Cup team.

Things weren't looking much better after the team took an overseas trip to China. The Americans lost two out of three friendlies to the Chinese, a strong team they knew would be tough to beat in the World Cup matches. And when the Chinese squad came to America, along with Norway, Team USA took only one of the four games.

This was not a good sign. Was the moment Mia had looked forward to her whole life going to be one big disappointment?

A lot of people thought so, but not Mia, and not her teammates. The U.S. squad knew they were struggling, but they were learning from every loss—learning what they needed to do better and learning the way their opponents played so they could take them down when it really counted. Mia felt like she was getting better every day in her new position as midfielder, and she had total faith in her supporting cast on the field, especially star Michelle Akers, who could pound the ball harder than anyone else in women's soccer.

Also, at the last minute Mia's best friend, Kristine Lilly, changed her mind and signed on for the World Cup. She had originally decided to stay at UNC instead of playing with the national team, so she had missed a lot of practice time and most of the friendlies. But when it came down to it, she couldn't stay away. Luckily Kristine was used to playing with everyone on the team, so she fit right in, playing opposite Mia at left midfield. With Kristine back at her side, Mia was more confident than ever that her team had what it took to make it to the top.

On November 17, 1991, the U.S. team faced their first challenge of the World Cup, an opening game against Sweden. Sweden played well, as always, but Mia's squad played better. Coach Dorrance told his players that they had to be aggressive if they wanted to win. The offense had to stop being cautious and start taking risks. They had to push toward their opponent's goal and trust the defense to take care of any problems. Following Dorrance's advice, the Americans powered their way to a 3–2 victory.

It was a great start and a big surprise to everyone who'd brushed off Team USA, assuming they wouldn't be a threat.

Some teams still figured it had just been a lucky break. They were sure the U.S. squad would be eliminated very soon.

But two days later the Americans crushed Brazil, 5–0, proving they were no one-hit wonder. Did anyone need to see more proof? No problem! How would a 3–0 win over Taiwan and then a gigantic 7–0 win over Taiwan do? Because Michelle Akers would be perfectly happy to pour in five goals in that second game against Taiwan, as she did very easily!

The excitement was building. The U.S. team was hot, and they knew it. Now they just had to keep it up. When they faced Germany on November 27, they were only one win away from the World Cup finals. Mia and Kristine worked their magic together against the tough German squad. They showed off their defensive abilities as they shut down all but two of Germany's attempts to make it to the goal, keeping the ball on the other end of the field for almost the entire game. Mia was especially proud to contribute on the defensive end because she'd finally become a complete player and it was a huge help to her team. With a final score of 5–2 Mia and her teammates squelched the Germans. They were going to the finals!

No one had believed the U.S. team would make it this far—except for the U.S. players themselves. But even they felt a little nervous about their chances in the final matchup. Team USA would have to battle Norway for the ultimate prize, and

Norway's squad was extremely talented and also held the mental edge—Norway had beaten the Americans in the last two games they played, both on U.S. home turf. Mia and her teammates arrived at Tianhe Stadium on November 30, slightly overwhelmed by what they faced that evening. But to their amazement, they soon discovered that the 65,000 mostly Chinese fans crammed into the stadium were cheering and screaming for *them,* not for the heavily favored Norway team. The support gave them the boost they needed to keep up their confidence, and they went into the game ready to win.

It wasn't long before Mia realized this game would be the toughest one yet. Norway had been paying attention to the way the Americans played in their other matches, and they came right back with their own powerful offense. Mia was like a whirl-wind on the field, seeming to be everywhere at once as she fought for control of the ball. But Norway's players struggled just as hard, and by halftime the score was tied at one goal apiece.

 The 1991 World Cup official report cited Mia as one of the best attacking defenders in the tournament.

The second half of the match stretched on without either team's offense managing to penetrate and score, but Norway

> **66**By winning [the 1991 women's World Cup], we
> kicked open the door for women's soccer and let in
> millions of girls who could now brag that American
> women were the best soccer players in the world.**99**
>
> —MIA HAMM

seemed to have the upper hand. They had the stamina to keep pushing and pushing, and they were happy to let the game go into overtime and get their win once the Americans were too exhausted to stop them. And sadly, it looked like that was about to happen, until Michelle Akers stepped in.

Michelle was watching every move the Norway players made, looking for her chance. When she spotted defender Tina Svensson about to pass the ball back to Norway's goalkeeper, Reiden Seth, she knew she'd found it. Svensson's play wasn't new, and it was usually pretty safe. Another defender was there to keep the ball protected, and once Seth got the ball, she could send it flying down the field away from their goal. But the five-foot-ten, 160-pound Michelle Akers was willing to give everything for a goal, as Svensson and the other defender found out when Michelle's body hurtled into Svensson's as she ran for the ball. The force of the impact knocked Svensson into her teammate and landed them both on the ground. Meanwhile

Svensson's concentration had been interrupted when she saw Michelle coming at her, and the result was a weak pass right before the crash of bodies.

Michelle kept chasing the ball, and since Seth had moved out of position to receive Svensson's pass, Michelle had a perfect shot. After another one of her famous strong kicks the U.S. team had taken the lead, 2–1. And with only three minutes left in the game, Norway couldn't recover. Mia and her teammates had done it—they'd won the first ever women's World Cup!

❝ *Winning in '91 was so cool because back then we were like a bunch of neighborhood kids who got together and played for the love of the sport.* ❞

—MIA HAMM

Chapter Five

Shooting Star

Mia was happier and prouder than she'd ever been in her life. She'd seen her dream come true—she'd been a part of making history! Not only had her team been the first to win a women's World Cup, but they were also the first American soccer team to win a world championship, since the American men never had. Talk about a trendsetter!

Still, life got back to normal pretty quickly. Even though Mia and her teammates had made such a huge accomplishment, the American sports world barely seemed to notice. "There were no TV crews or fans waiting for us at the airport when we returned," Mia shares. "*Sports Illustrated* chose to note the historic victory with a tiny mention in its scorecard section, and newspapers across the country buried the story next to the tire ads in the back."

What?! That was it? Mia couldn't help feeling frustrated that the media were giving so little attention to their win. It wasn't

A set of trading cards was created for publicity for the 1994 men's World Cup, and Mia was one of a small number of women players who got her own card!

that she cared about the fame or glory, which had never been important to her. She'd hoped that winning the women's World Cup would finally help women's soccer become more popular in her home country so that little girls everywhere could get psyched about playing. But even though there wasn't exactly tons of fanfare, Mia knew this was just the beginning. She was already gearing up for the next World Cup, in 1995, and as determined as ever to convince the United States to support women's soccer.

What Mia did bring back to America—along with her medal—was a stronger sense than ever of what she could do. Now that she was back at UNC, she couldn't wait to work in everything she'd learned during her time with the national team. While Mia had been away, the Tar Heels had claimed their sixth straight championship, and Mia was ready to help them get their seventh in 1992. Her teammate April Heinrichs believed it was a sure bet. "I've seen a new, improved version of Mia since the World Cup," April said. "Her confidence level is higher. Her consistency is better."

The Tar Heels zoomed through the regular season, racking up victories. They finished with a perfect record of 22 wins and 0 losses. "It was an exciting and special group," Mia says of that year's squad. She was a major reason for that, turning in top-level play on both ends of the field. Of the 25 college games Mia played in 1992, she scored an amazing 32 goals and made 33 assists, shocking soccer fans with her huge numbers. No other women's soccer player had done as much in one season as she did that year.

After wrapping up their excellent season, UNC faced the Duke Blue Devils in the ACC championship game. Even though the Tar Heels had dominated all year long, they knew they couldn't let their guard down. Duke was a tough team, with a record almost as good as North Carolina's. But what Duke *didn't* have was Mia Hamm—and that was about to make all the difference.

 The Tar Heels outscored their opponents a total of 132–11 over the entire 1992 season.

Mia had said before the ACC championship that she'd come away from the World Cup with "a much better understanding of what it takes to be a playmaker." She knew she

Mia set an NCAA record with a total of 278 career points at UNC.

could score goals when it counted, but she also knew that sometimes the smarter move was to set up a teammate for a better shot. That year she had led the nation in assists as well as scoring, and this newly developed strength was crucial in the ACC matchup against Duke. Each of the three goals UNC made against Duke that day were off of brilliant passes from Mia. She never let up on Duke, charging them for the ball until she got her way. After Duke tied the game at 1–1 early in the second half, Mia held on to her confidence, making sure her teammates did as well. The payoff came after two more goals, assisted by Mia, gave UNC the win, with a final score of 3–1.

Duke was eager for a rematch, and they played hard to qualify for the NCAA finals so they could meet UNC one more time that year. UNC was ready for them, but they were in for a surprise when the Blue Devils took a one-point lead 17 minutes into the game. Mia rallied her teammates not to be intimidated and to fight back with everything they had. And wow—that turned out to be more than anyone ever imagined!

Ten minutes after Duke's goal Mia scored one of her own to tie the match. Then within minutes Mia's teammate Keri Sanchez scored again while Mia and Kristine Lilly kept the Duke defense distracted. The Blue Devils had barely caught their breath when Mia slammed in another goal, followed by one more from her teammate. With lightning speed UNC had galloped past Duke to a 4–1 lead.

And it didn't stop there!

As UNC unbelievably continued to score goal after goal in the second half, Coach Dorrance pulled Mia from the game, not wanting to risk her getting injured when the win was almost guaranteed. The score was 7–1 when Mia asked to go back in. This was her best friend Kristine Lilly's last game as a Tar Heel since Kristine was graduating this year, and Mia wanted to be by her side for the final minutes of the match. Dorrance relented, and Mia kicked in her third goal of the game.

---

66 *She's probably the best women's soccer player in the world. She showed us that today.* 99

—DUKE COACH BILL HEMPEN,
AFTER UNC's 1992 ACC CHAMPIONSHIP WIN

The final score was a mind-blowing 9–1 win for the Tar Heels. Not only did UNC have their seventh straight NCAA championship title, but they had pulled off a breathtaking stunt on Fetzer Field that day. "We all pushed one another to be better," Mia said later, "and we achieved something in the NCAA championship game that will never be done again. . . . That NCAA title my junior year remains among my greatest triumphs on the soccer field."

Mia's standout play with UNC that fall didn't go unnoticed. She received every vote for U.S. Soccer Female Athlete of the Year and took home the MVP awards for both the ACC and NCAA tournaments. Mia's star was on the rise, and she knew she was exactly where she wanted to be—right at the top of her game.

❝ In terms of offense, [the 1992 Tar Heels squad] was probably the most dynamic team Anson [Dorrance] has ever had, and that's saying a lot. ❞

—MIA HAMM

But when Mia rejoined the national team for a trio of games that spring against Denmark, Norway, and Germany, she realized she couldn't afford to get overconfident. Now that the rest of the world knew what the American women could do, they were working extra hard to find out how to beat them. The U.S. team defeated Denmark, 2–0, but lost to both Norway and

Germany, 1–0. They stumbled again at the World University Games over the summer of 1993, losing to China in the finals. Mia knew that her team would have to shape up in the next two years if they wanted to repeat as World Cup champs in 1995. And they definitely wanted that!

In the meantime Mia still had one more year at UNC. She took her role on the Tar Heels as seriously as ever, leading them to another undefeated season. Facing Duke again in the ACC championship, Mia reminded the Blue Devils why she'd become their nightmare a year before. Her three second-half goals brought UNC the win and the ACC title.

Next the team was on to the NCAA championship, where UNC was up against George Mason University. Mia played her last college game with a heart full of emotion but still displayed her usual stunning speed and grace on the field. After putting in the Tar Heels' fourth goal of the game and then facing the crowd's standing ovation, Mia was overwhelmed. UNC won the game 6–0, giving Mia the perfect parting gift—one last NCAA championship title. Not long after, she was named National Player of the Year for the second time in a row.

"This is my field of dreams," Mia said about Chapel Hill's Fetzer Field as she prepared to leave UNC. But as much as Mia loved being a Tar Heel, she was ready to move on. "I've had some wonderful years here," she shared, "but I don't want to sit and look at all the trophies. I don't want to live in the past—I want to live now!"

Mia had more reason than ever to look forward to the future. During her 1993 season with the Tar Heels she and her teammates had found out some incredible news. Since many of them shared an apartment together off campus, they all heard the info at the same time, with one phone call—women's soccer had been added to the summer Olympics as a full medal sport! That meant that in 1996, when the Olympic Games would be held in Atlanta, Georgia—right here in her home country—Mia could compete for an Olympic gold medal!

"I grew up on the Olympics," she gushed, sharing her happiness at being able to play in the games. "You hear all the clichés, that it's a dream come true. Well, it is, for myself and for every young girl growing up playing any sport."

Suddenly everything Mia had wished for seemed to be coming true. The 1994 men's World Cup was being held in the United States for the first time ever, bringing new attention to the sport of soccer here at home. And with the women gearing up to compete in the 1996 Olympics, the media finally started to hype the women's soccer players, focusing mostly on Mia.

Shy, humble Mia, who was always so quick to give the credit to someone else, was right there in the spotlight. She was even offered an endorsement deal with Nike to help them advertise their cleats. Mia would have been perfectly happy *not* to have her name and face out there, but she did it for one reason—she saw it as the chance to finally promote women's soccer to little girls across the country. "It's very important for young girls to have female athletes with whom they can identify," Mia explained.

And now that she was a role model for girls everywhere, the big question was—could Mia and her teammates hold on to their World Cup title in 1995?

❝*The goals and the championships are nice, but the emotions, the tears, the smiles on my teammates' faces are my championships.*❞

—MIA HAMM

Chapter Six

Golden Girl

The year 1994 was a very busy one for Mia. Not only was she getting ready for her battle for the next World Cup, but she was also preparing for her wedding. That December, Mia married her college sweetheart, Christiaan Corey, a marine pilot.

Of course, Mia had to squeeze her dress fittings in between practices with the U.S. squad. The American team was working harder than ever, anxious to get in shape for the 1995 World Cup. Teams across the world were shaping up with one goal in mind—to take down the reigning champs.

Mia and her teammates had it a little easier this time around—they were being paid a salary for their work on the World Cup team after having proved they deserved it at the last tournament. But unfortunately the squad was facing several challenges from the inside. Longtime coach Anson Dorrance had announced in 1994 that it was no longer possible to juggle his responsibilities coaching both the women's team at UNC and the national squad. Since his heart was with the Tar Heels, he stayed there and handed the U.S. team over to new coach Tony DiCiccio. DiCiccio was a strong coach and popular with the players, but it was still an adjustment for Mia and her teammates to get used to working with someone other than Dorrance.

---

66 *When Mia is on, there's no one better in the world.* 99

—TONY DICICCIO

The next blow came when Michelle Akers was diagnosed with chronic fatigue syndrome, a serious disease that can leave its victims barely able to get out of bed. Michelle was fighting with everything she had to stay in the game, but she no longer had the same energy that had powered the team to their 1991 victory.

Still, even with these unexpected difficulties the U.S. team went into the World Cup looking strong, winning nine straight matches leading up to the opening game of the tournament on June 6. Hot off their streak, they had high hopes of beating China that day. But the game ended in a tie, 3–3. It wasn't a loss, but it also wasn't a win, and now if China went on to win more of their upcoming matches than the Americans did, the U.S. team would be in danger of not making the final round.

Game two was against Denmark, and the U.S. players started to relax when their 2–0 lead seemed solid with only six minutes left on the clock. But then the team received a scary blow—the referee ejected their goalkeeper, Briana Scurry, from the game. Scurry had accidentally stepped over the edge of the penalty box with the ball in her hands, and she was called for intentionally handling the ball outside of the area where a goal-keeper is allowed to use her hands.

Mia was listed as the third-string goalkeeper for the U.S. team, but it was never expected that she'd actually have to play the position. Then the team's assistant coach, April Heinrichs, called Mia over to the sideline. "She put her arm around me," Mia recalls, "and said very calmly, because I'm sure she didn't want to freak me out, 'Mia, we've used all our substitutes, and we're going to put you in goal. How do you feel about that?'" At first Mia didn't get it—they still had two players on the bench who actually *played* goalkeeper. Then Heinrichs's words sank in—the team had used up their substitutions, and they couldn't bring anyone else out on the field. It had to be Mia.

Taking over as the last line of defense for her team was scary enough, but even worse, Mia's first job would be to block a free kick from 19 yards out. "Yes, my international goal-keeping debut was to face a free kick about as close to the goal as could be without it being a penalty shot," Mia says, "from a woman who would like nothing better than to blast me halfway across the Atlantic."

Mia held her breath as Denmark's Kamma Flaeng began her run toward the ball. Would she be able to stop it? Luckily she didn't have to find out because Flaeng's kick flew over the net. But Mia's goal-keeping ability *was* tested for real during the final seconds of the game. When she saw the ball coming toward her, Mia sucked it up and took the impact on her stomach, a brutal save that assured the United States' victory moments later. Mia was just relieved not to have cost her team anything. "The goal is so much bigger when you're inside it than when you're shooting at it!" Mia marveled later.

❝*I've got to admit that I'm addicted to winning and have been fortunate enough to win a lot of games in my life.*❞

—MIA HAMM

Now the U.S. team would move on to play Australia, at the same time that China was facing down Denmark. To claim the top spot in the next round, the American players had to win their game *and* score more goals than China scored against Denmark because the number of goals scored would serve as

Mia's senior yearbook photo

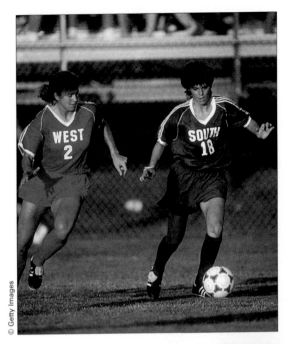

Mia (right) fights for the ball during a match at the U.S. Olympic Festival in 1989.

© Getty Images

In her individual team picture from the 1993 World Cup

© Rick Stewart/Getty Images

Going for the ball in an Olympic match against Sweden in 1996

Mia (center) breaks away from defenders Marina Dikareva (left) and Tatiana Egorova (right) during a 1998 game against the Russian women's soccer team.

A player from Team China falls victim to Mia's tough defensive moves in the 1999 Women's World Cup Final.

Holding up the World Cup trophy after Team USA's win in 1999

Practicing with friend and Team USA teammate Kristine Lilly in preparation for
Portugal's Algarve Cup and, ultimately, for the 2000 Olympic Games

Mia (left) and Steffi Jones of the Washington Freedom battle the Carolina Courage's Tiffany Roberts for the ball during the WUSA Championship in 2002.

Celebrating after scoring a goal in the 2002 WUSA Championship

the tiebreaker. So while the U.S. team played their game, the squad's liaison was getting constant updates on how China was doing. Every time the United States heard that China had scored another goal, they needed to match it with one of their own. Team USA had secured a 3–1 lead over Australia, and it looked like the match was theirs, but then the cell phone rang. They had to notch one more goal in order to top the number of goals the Chinese had made in their win over Denmark! They were trying to beat two teams at once, including one team they weren't actually playing against. But the Americans came through with another goal, meaning they'd play Japan instead of the tougher Sweden team in the quarterfinals.

As they'd hoped, the U.S. team easily crushed Japan, 4–0. But before they could reach the finals, they had to meet their rival Norway in the semifinals. The Norway players were still stinging from the 1991 defeat, and they'd spent the past four years determined to see things end differently this time. The hard work paid off, and Norway won the game with just one goal that the U.S. squad failed to match. Mia and her teammates were devastated and couldn't hold back their tears. The Americans went on to beat China 2–0, giving the U.S. third place in the tournament behind second-place Germany and Norway, who took the cup. But nothing other than first place could satisfy Mia—not when she knew her team was good enough to get it.

The World Cup had barely ended when Mia and the rest of Team USA began gearing up for the 1996 summer Olympics. They had an extra motivation to win in Atlanta now that they'd lost their World Cup title. "Everyone committed themselves to...being fitter, to being faster, to being stronger, and bringing the team closer together, on the field and off," Mia shares. "We had a renewed dedication after [the 1995 World Cup]—we saw our shortcomings and focused on our weaknesses."

The whole team actually moved in together in January 1996, living and training in Orlando, Florida. Every second possible was spent on nailing down their technique and strategy to ensure a gold medal the following summer. "I've worked too hard and too long to let anything stand in the way of my goals," Mia told a reporter. "I will not let my team down and I will not let myself down. I'm going to break myself in half to make sure [we win the medal]."

Mia's teammates got scared that she'd broken something for real when she took a bad fall during a game against Germany in late March. But thankfully, her injury turned out to be a sprained knee. After just a few weeks of rest she could rejoin her friends on the field.

Mia was plenty rested and back to full strength by the time the opening game of the summer Olympics rolled around on July 21, 1996. The Olympic Games were based in Atlanta, but soccer matches were played in different locations, and this one was in familiar territory for the American team—Orlando, Florida. Approximately 25,000 fans filled the stadium, at the time the largest crowd in history to attend a women's soccer match. They were even willing to brave the incredible 100-degree temperature—maybe because they weren't the ones who had to play soccer in that heat!

Mia didn't let the hot sun stand in her way, though. She showed the fans what her team could do, turning in one goal and one assist to help the United States to their 3–0 victory over Denmark. It wasn't just her scoring that made everyone's eyes bulge—no one could believe her speed. Finally a hometown crowd was getting a glimpse of what made Mia so special, her ability to tear down the field and leave the opposition in the dust. "Every time she got the ball she was dangerous," Coach DiCiccio said after the game. "She was the key player for us. Mia took the game over."

---

66 *We made a little mistake, and [Mia] said, 'Thank you' and scored.* 99
—DENMARK'S COACH KELD GANTZHORN,
AFTER THE OPENING GAME OF THE 1996 OLYMPICS

Unfortunately, when the Americans went up against Sweden two days later, Mia's reputation was no help. Sweden agreed that she was "dangerous" and did everything they could to shut her down, including knocking her to the ground repeatedly. On one play Mia's teammates waited for her to get up . . . and kept waiting. Mia struggled to stand but was heartbroken to realize that something was very wrong. When she was finally brought out of the game and checked out by a doctor, she received the bad news—she had a sprained left ankle.

The United States still beat Sweden, 2–1, and Mia knew her team had plenty of talented players without her. But she couldn't bear the idea of watching the rest of the matches from the sidelines. She sat out the Americans' next game, against China, frustrated to see the two teams stuck in a dead heat. The game ended in a scoreless tie, so both teams moved on to the next round.

Team USA was scheduled to play Norway in the semifinals on July 28. Mia was in a lot of pain, but there was no way she would miss that game. She was taking Norway down this time! Coach DiCiccio allowed her back in the starting lineup, warning her to go easy and focus on distracting Norway's defense from her teammates. Mia did the best she could, taking tons of assaults and playing every minute of the game. Still, Norway scored an early goal and held on to the one-point lead for most of the game. Then as the clock wound down, Mia pushed hard and got the ball into the penalty area. Once again she was knocked down, but this time the referee called a penalty. The Americans would have a chance to score!

Michelle Akers, still able to come through when it counted, stepped up to take the penalty kick. She made the shot, sending the game into overtime. Inspired by Mia's and Michelle's last minute heroics, midfielder Julie Foudy assisted Shannon MacMillan on the game-winning overtime goal. The Americans were going to the Olympic gold medal match!

The record of 25,000 fans at the opening women's soccer match of the 1996 Olympics was shattered just a couple of weeks later when 76,000 people packed the stands to watch the Americans face China in the gold medal match.

Mia was absolutely ecstatic. She and her teammates had faced down their biggest rival, and now they had a chance to reclaim the status of world champs. Only one thing stood in their way—the Chinese team, who wanted that gold medal just as badly.

When the two teams met for the final round on August 1, China made it clear they were there to fight. They played the

Americans aggressively, and the score was tied at one goal apiece at halftime. Even though Mia had helped Shannon MacMillan make her team's goal, she started to worry that she was hurting her team since she couldn't play at full speed. She even asked her teammates if they thought she should sit out. Seeing her team win the gold medal meant much more to Mia than her own desire to be out there playing. But everyone told Mia she was crazy to think they'd be better off without her, even with her injury. And it didn't take long for Mia to pull off a move that proved her friends right.

Roughly halfway into the second period Mia expertly set up her teammates Joy Fawcett and Tiffeny Milbrett, shooting a perfect pass to Fawcett that Fawcett angled to Milbrett for a direct attempt on the goal. *Score!*

The goal held, and when the time ran out, the U.S. team had won, 2–1. The Americans had made history for the second time— they'd won the first ever Olympic gold medal in women's soccer!

Chapter Seven

The Pressure Is On

Mia felt like she was walking on air—nothing could bring her down. She had seen her ultimate dream come true, and she'd helped her squad reach that dream as a real team player, without even scoring an actual goal herself. "Mia impacts the game whether she scores or not," her teammate Brandi Chastain confirmed after the game. "She tears defenses apart. She is awesome."

Mia was only a little disappointed that her throbbing ankle, which had finally given out on her 60 seconds before the end of the golden game, wouldn't let her join her teammates for their victory run around the field. She was flanked by her team's trainers while her friends jogged the lap, waving to all their screaming fans. As soon as the squad finished their run, they were at Mia's side, surrounding her, and Mia got to share the precious moment with the women who'd been wanting this as badly as she had.

Later she shared her excitement with someone else special in her life—her brother Garrett, who was prouder than anyone else in the stands that day. Having Garrett there to see her Olympic triumph was especially meaningful to Mia for a very sad reason—Garrett was ill, and he was getting sicker all the time. Mia and Garrett had always been extremely close, and she was devastated when he was diagnosed with aplastic anemia, a potentially life-threatening disease. She had always believed he would find a way to beat it, but now it was becoming apparent that Garrett didn't have a lot of time.

In 1997 a donor was finally found who could give Garrett the bone marrow that was his only chance. The transplant took place, and at first Garrett improved. But he soon became very sick again, and he died that spring.

---

66 *Garrett was, and always will be, my inspiration. Now, no matter where I play, I feel Garrett is there.* 99

—MIA HAMM

Mia had never experienced anything like the pain she felt then, losing one of the people she loved most in the world. "I've been blessed by so many things," she shared, "but I would give them all back to have him."

It was almost like Mia didn't even know how to go on, how to put one foot in front of the other and keep living her life without her brother there to share everything. But slowly she realized that she needed to, for Garrett as well as for herself. "The athletic field is where Garrett and I had so many great moments together, and I knew he would have wanted me out there," Mia later explained. "I knew also one of the best ways to deal with my grief was to play and be with my teammates."

 Garrett's initials are on the bottom of every pair of Mia's line of Nike shoes.

The bond that Mia shared with the other members of Team USA both on and off the field had never meant so much to her before. "My teammates were remarkable in caring for me and my family," she says. "There's no way I could have come back without their support and love, and I will always be grateful."

Along with playing the best soccer she could, Mia realized there was another way she could honor her brother's memory. The media attention on women's soccer was like nothing she'd ever seen before in her life. Unlike after the 1991 World Cup, when no one back home even seemed to *know* she was a world champion, the 1996 Olympics had made Mia a star. Gatorade had decided, like Nike, to "just do it" and hire Mia to endorse their products. Mia couldn't resist the chance to star in a commercial with her all-time sports idol, Michael Jordan. The theme of the commercial was "anything you can do, I can do better" as the two athletes squared off against each other in different sports. Mia got a special thrill out of the fact that during the filming, she actually held her own against His Airness himself during the basketball sequence! The commercial was a big success, and Tom Fox, vice president of sports marketing at Gatorade, stated that "until Mia came along, everyone thought that Gatorade was a male brand. Not anymore."

Go, Mia!

But along with the excitement of seeing women's soccer gain focus and popularity in her home country, Mia realized she could use her new status to help others who were stricken with the disease that had taken her brother's life. She created the Mia Hamm Foundation to raise money for research and awareness about aplastic anemia. And whenever she handed out autographs, she included information about the illness and how easy it is to get tested to see if you can save someone's life. Mia also established an annual Garrett Game to raise money for the cause, and her teammates were right there at her side, supporting her every step (and kick!) of the way.

Even with her new roles as a spokesperson for women's soccer and aplastic anemia—two issues very close to her heart—Mia was still first and foremost a soccer player. As she began to heal from losing Garrett, she set her sights on the upcoming challenges for her team, starting with the Goodwill Games in 1998.

The U.S. team was once again playing on home turf, this time in Long Island, New York. Mia had been working hard to regain her concentration, and she couldn't wait to get out there and show Garrett she was going to keep on winning for him. Coach DiCiccio also warned his team that it was especially crucial for them to win this tournament because the next World Cup was coming up soon and was scheduled to take place in America this time. "We don't want China, or any other team, to feel they can beat us here [in the United States]," he explained.

Mia listened and obviously took her coach's words seriously. In the semifinal matchup against Denmark she let loose, scoring three of the Americans' five goals. Team USA shut down their opponents, keeping Denmark from making even one goal. Now it was on to the finals, a rematch against China.

The Chinese team did everything they could to end up on top this time, and after 66 minutes the score was still stuck at 0–0. "China is a great team," Mia later wrote in her book, *Go for the Goal: A Champion's Guide to Winning in Soccer and Life.* "You are not going to get many chances to score against them, and when you do, they have an almost unbeatable goalkeeper." *Almost* is the key word there, and as long as there's a chance, Mia will take it.

In the sixty-sixth minute Mia got a pass from Kristine Lilly, and she rushed the goal. "I raced in one-on-one on the Chinese goalkeeper and drilled my shot into the left corner," Mia remembers. "I savor that goal because I got one chance near the end of the game and nailed it."

But one just wasn't enough for Mia. With only three minutes left in the game, she scored again. It was another win and another shutout, with a final score of 2–0. *Plus* Mia had another gold medal—the Americans had won the Goodwill Games tournament!

❝*Mia turned in a Michael Jordan–like performance tonight.*❞

—COACH DICICCIO,
AFTER THE GOODWILL GAMES FINAL MATCH AGAINST CHINA

Then Mia realized something else—those two game-winning goals against China had also been her ninety-sixth and ninety-seventh career goals. She was getting close to a magical 100 goals! Two more goals in a game against Mexico brought her to 99. Now it was just a question of when it would happen.

At the same time that Mia was gunning for her 100th goal, two American baseball players, Sammy Sosa and Mark McGwire, were competing to beat Roger Maris's home-run record. When Mia arrived in Rochester, New York, in September for a game against Russia, she noticed someone in the stands had a sign that said, McGwire 63, Sosa 63, Hamm 99. The media picked up on the comparison and gave it some attention, and Mia was psyched to see women's soccer right up there with baseball, the classic American sport.

Maybe the sign was a good luck charm because that night against Russia, Mia did it—she scored her 100th career goal! "I was so excited all I could do was run," she later wrote. "The players and coaches on the bench emptied onto the field, and everyone mobbed me as if I'd just scored the winning goal in the World Cup."

Mia's team captain, Carla Overbeck, handed her the ball she'd scored with, and the crowd cheered like crazy. Mia was overwhelmed and thrilled but as always wanted to let people know that she shared the accomplishment with her teammates. "The crowd was great and it was a lot of fun," she said, "but it was even better because I could share it with my teammates. It's a credit to this team that we can have moments like this."

The U.S. squad seemed stronger than ever, and they were dead set on being the first women's soccer team to achieve a "triple"—holding the Olympic, Goodwill Games, and World Cup titles at the same time. It didn't look like anything could stop them, and their country was behind them more than ever before.

But for the first time Mia realized there was a flip side to all of the media attention. It was great to have little girls look at her as a role model and know that she could inspire them to become soccer players themselves. And she and her teammates loved having so many fans cheer for them the way they never had before. But along with the support came expectations. Now if Mia made a mistake, she wouldn't just be letting herself and her teammates down, but an entire country of people. Plus corporations were starting to invest money in sponsoring women's soccer, so there was a lot on the line if Mia didn't come through.

 Mia was named one of *People* magazine's 50 Most Beautiful People in 1997.

The winter and early spring months of 1999 were tough on Mia. Her husband, Christiaan, had to spend a six-month tour of duty in Japan, so he couldn't be with her on the second anniversary of Garrett's death. Mia suffered an eight-game stretch without scoring a single goal, and some began to wonder if she and the rest of the U.S. team would crack under all the pressure. The squad had never competed with so many people counting on them before, and this time they'd be fighting for the World Cup title right here on home turf. Could the Americans really do it with everyone's eyes on them?

Then on May 22, 1999, Mia reminded everyone whom they were dealing with. She scored her 108th career goal, topping the world record—for men *and* women—of 107 held by a retired Italian player. Humble as ever, Mia said she wished it could have been her teammate Michelle Akers breaking the record because she knew it would have been if Michelle hadn't been suffering from chronic fatigue syndrome. But it was still an exciting moment, and it gave Mia exactly the boost of confidence she needed for her next challenge—the 1999 World Cup!

Chapter | Eight

Back on Top

The U.S. team's first game of the 1999 World Cup was played against Denmark on June 19, at Giants Stadium in New Jersey. Mia and her teammates arrived in New Jersey a week early to start their training camp and get psyched for the tournament. This time they were getting tons of press, and David Letterman even had Mia's teammate Brandi Chastain on his late night talk show.

But even though Mia knew her team had more fans than ever before, she was still shocked by what she saw when the team bus pulled into Giants Stadium. "There were thousands of people with their faces painted, waving flags, holding balloons, wearing our jerseys, and carrying signs," she recalls. "For the first time, we felt as if the whole nation was behind us."

It was an intense wave of emotion for Mia, and she couldn't help thinking back to her first World Cup, "before we had web

> **❝** *It was like we had achieved something we had worked for our whole lives and the game hadn't even started yet!* **❞**
>
> —MIA HAMM, ON THE AMAZING TURNOUT OF SUPPORT FOR HER TEAM AT THE OPENING GAME OF THE 1999 WORLD CUP

sites dedicated to us, before we got fan mail by the bushel, and before our games were on TV." It was incredible for Mia to see how far women's soccer had come in America, and the moment was huge for her. But her purpose today was the same as it had been during all the games she'd played in with far less attention from fans or the media—to win.

Mia got started early, scoring the first goal of the competition—and the first goal of the World Cup!—17 minutes into the match. The entire stadium went crazy, and Mia and her teammates were more pumped than ever. In the second half Mia assisted Julie Foudy on the next American goal, and Kristine Lilly kicked in the third. Team USA was off to a great start, with a 3–0 victory over Denmark!

Their next game was against Nigeria, and it was held at Soldier Field in Chicago. The Nigerian team scored in the first few minutes of the game, shocking the fans and giving the Americans a little wake-up call. But the U.S. squad came back with a vengeance. First they scored three goals in a five-minute span. Mia assisted on the first and pounded the second one in herself. Then as the game continued, three more goals brought them to a lead of 6–1 at halftime. Mia sat out most of the second half, cheering Tiffeny Milbrett on when she scored the squad's seventh goal.

The team followed up the win with another against North Korea, 3–0, and moved on to the quarterfinals against Germany.

Mia was psyched to find out that the quarterfinal game would take place at Jack Kent Cooke Stadium, outside Washington, D.C. The stadium was home to her favorite football team, the Washington Redskins, and wasn't too far from the town in Virginia where she'd spent her last year of high school. Now Mia had an extra reason to make sure her team came out on top of this match—to give one of her hometowns something to be proud of!

Ten percent of the price of every 1999 women's World Cup ticket bought with a MasterCard was donated to the Mia Hamm Foundation.

Unfortunately things didn't get off to a great start. Mia came into the game with a pulled muscle in her left hip. She could still play, but she was in a lot of pain. And the pain in her hip was nothing next to what she felt when she saw what happened in the first five minutes on the field.

Through a terrible misunderstanding between Brandi Chastain and U.S. goalkeeper Briana Scurry, Brandi ended up scoring a goal—*for Germany!*

Now the United States was down by one, and their confidence had been hurt. But they reminded themselves that they were a strong team and could easily come back as long as they believed in themselves. Besides, they couldn't let down the very important family that was sitting in the stands, having made the trip from their home address at 1600 Pennsylvania Avenue. That's right, President Bill Clinton, along with his wife, Hillary, and their daughter, Chelsea, were all watching the game. So the Americans really had to show their stuff today. Soon they'd tied the score at 1–1, but Germany rebounded and netted a goal of their own before halftime.

When the second half of the game started, Team USA got down to business. Brandi, still angry at herself for her part in Germany's first goal, went all out to give the Americans their second, bringing the game to a 2–2 tie. All it took was one more goal, contributed by Joy Fawcett off of Shannon MacMillan's assist, and the U.S. squad had taken the game, 3–2!

Mia and her teammates were celebrating in the locker room when the first family themselves came in to join them.

President Clinton made sure to shake every player's hand, congratulating each one on her hard work. Mia felt like she would burst with pride. Over the years she had seen so many dreams come true, and now—watching the president of the United States standing there congratulating the members of her team—she was living out one more.

But even with all the excitement, the World Cup title wasn't back in Mia's hands yet, and she wouldn't be satisfied until it was.

The U.S. squad was up against Brazil next in the semifinals, and Mia and her teammates charged forward, set on making it to the final round this time. Brazil fought hard but fell to the Americans, 2–0.

Yes—Mia was going to get her chance to be a World Cup champion again! All she and her team had to do was win one more game and the title was theirs. They were playing China, the team they'd taken the Olympic gold medal from three years before. Were they up for a repeat performance? It was time to find out.

"On July 10, 1999," Mia later wrote, "we stepped onto the field at the Rose Bowl to face off against China for the World Cup final in what was one of the greatest moments of my career." An astounding 90,000 fans filled the stands, a record crowd in America for any women's sporting event. But as awesome as it felt for Mia to see so many fans, she also knew just how crushed she'd be if she let them down. There was no way the U.S. team was leaving that stadium with second place.

China turned out to be just as determined, and the game stretched on and on without either team scoring a goal. Finally the whistle blew, and the teams were still locked at 0–0. Since World Cup games can't end in a tie, the game went into overtime.

Fifteen minutes passed, and *still* no one scored. A Chinese player came close, and Mia could barely breathe as she watched the ball fly toward the goal. But a header from Kristine Lilly saved the day, and the exhausted players were forced into an incredible *second* overtime.

❝ *She wanted the responsibility. She wanted the ball. That's the quality of player and person Mia is. As a coach, you can't measure how important it is for your star player to be such a leader and a character person.* **❞**

—COACH DICICCIO

Both the U.S. team and China continued to play hard, and when the minutes of the second overtime period ran out, the game was still tied at 0–0.

Now this game—the one that meant everything to Mia— would be decided on penalty kicks. Each team chose five players to take shots from the penalty spot on the field, and whichever team made more of their kicks would be the next World Cup champions. Mia was terrified because so much could easily go wrong. She really started to freak when she was told that she'd be kicking fourth for her team, because she knew that penalty kicks weren't her best skill. What if she missed? She alone would have the power to lose this game for her team and her country.

Mia watched as her teammates Carla Overbeck and Joy Fawcett made their kicks. The first two Chinese players also made theirs, so the teams were tied, 2–2.

Mia's nerves were racing, and she knew it was almost her turn out there. All she needed was . . .

Wait a second—did that just happen? Mia's whole face lit up, and she—along with everyone else at the Rose Bowl—went crazy. China's third kicker, Liu Ying, had missed her shot! Briana Scurry, U.S. goalkeeper extraordinaire, had correctly guessed which direction Ying would send the ball, and she'd managed to swat it out of the net. Now as long as the rest of the U.S. players made their kicks, they'd win the game!

Kristine Lilly was up next, and Mia's heart soared as she watched the ball go in. China scored on their next attempt, and then it was all up to Mia.

Staying as calm as she could, she walked up to the ball and went for it. Later she admitted she honestly couldn't even remember that moment. Her whole body was so keyed up that she was just on autopilot. But the most natural thing in the world for Mia Hamm was to kick that ball into the net, and sure enough, she did it!

Brandi Chastain was the last U.S. player to shoot, and the second Mia saw Brandi's foot connect with the ball, she knew the kick was good. Seconds later it was official—the Americans were again the World Cup champions! They'd achieved an unimaginable triple, topping their recent Olympic and Goodwill Games victories with this one, the sweetest championship of all.

 Mia and her teammates painted their fingernails and toenails red, white, and blue for the World Cup games.

The fanfare following the Americans' World Cup win was like nothing Mia had ever experienced. She couldn't stop crying during the awards ceremony, where she and her teammates were presented with their medals and the World Cup trophy. But the tears disappeared when it was time to film their commercial for Disneyland, a tradition for champion sports teams in America that now finally included women's soccer.

People, Newsweek, Time, and *Sports Illustrated* all featured the World Cup champs on their covers the same week. It was only the second time in history that the four magazines had spotlighted the same cover story in one week!

The U.S. team was treated to another visit from President Clinton back in the locker room, and that was just the beginning. Suddenly the players were in demand everywhere, going from a victory parade in Disneyland to interviews on the morning talk shows in New York. A photo of the entire team was shot for the cover of *People* magazine, and even though by then Mia and some of her teammates had been on magazine covers before, this one was Mia's favorite because it featured them all together.

While they were in New York, Mia and a few teammates went to the world-famous sports arena Madison Square Garden to watch the WNBA All-Star game. They were introduced during a time-out and received a standing ovation from the sold-out crowd. The basketball players themselves even broke from their huddle to clap along with the fans!

After New York came a ceremony in Washington, D.C., at the White House and then an invitation to watch the launch of the first shuttle flight commanded by a woman down in Cape Canaveral, Florida.

Mia and her teammates had done it. They'd brought women's soccer to center stage in their home country. It was all really happening—everything Mia had dreamed of. Well, *almost* everything. There was still one more piece missing, but Mia was about to find out it was just around the corner!

Chapter Nine

Freedom Fighter

As much as Mia loved international competition, she'd always wished women's soccer could be a big enough deal in America that the sport could have its own national professional league, like the WNBA for women's basketball. And in 2000 it finally happened—the first American women's soccer league was established, the Women's United Soccer Association (WUSA).

Mia, along with many of her teammates on the national squad, got to be founding members of the newly created teams. Just how many "first evers" could Mia be a part of? Obviously she was up for as many as possible!

❝*I can kick and throw like Mia Hamm.*❞

—WOMEN'S WORLD CUP SOCCER BARBIE

To make things fair, the top players on Team USA were split up among the eight teams. Mia ended up with the Washington Freedom, and she was excited to play for a team with a home base near her old stomping ground in Virginia.

But before the WUSA could get off the ground, the U.S. national team had one more event to tackle together—the 2000 Summer Olympics in Sydney, Australia, where they hoped to repeat as gold medalists.

The Americans were definitely the favored team going into the tournament. They were the current world champions from both the World Cup *and* the last Olympic games and hey, they had Mia Hamm!

 Nike sells more than four times as many Mia Hamm soccer jerseys as they do for any other soccer star, male or female.

Mia came through for the team, as expected. First she scored one of the U.S. team's two goals against Norway in the opening match, with Tiffeny Milbrett putting in the other to give the Americans a 2–0 victory. Later Mia went on to notch the only—and game-winning—goal in the semifinal match against Brazil.

In an interesting twist, the gold medal game ended up squaring off the two teams whose match had opened the Olympic soccer games—America and Norway. And Mia and Tiffeny, the heroes of that earlier match against Norway, got off to an early start here, with Mia giving Tiffeny an assist on the first goal just five minutes into play. But Norway was tired of seeing the United States win, and they felt they were the team who could beat them. After all, they'd done it before when it counted, at the 1995 World Cup. And they'd done it more often in international competition than any other team.

The Americans knew they were in for a battle when Norway knotted the score at 1–1 before halftime. But when Norway upped the ante to 2–1 in the second half, the U.S. team started to get nervous. They were playing hard, and Mia seemed to be everywhere at once, but the team just couldn't get another goal. Then in the final seconds of regulation time, Mia and Tiffeny did it again as Mia assisted on Tiffeny's second goal of the game. Now the match would go into sudden death over-time—whichever team scored first would win the game and the gold medal!

Unfortunately that team was Norway. There was some controversy over Norway's goal because the ball touched the shoulder of the player who kicked it in, but the referees let it stand. Norway had won the gold medal.

The Americans had still won an Olympic silver medal, but it was hard for Mia to be happy with that. Not when she and her teammates knew they could have done better. But their coach, April Heinrichs—who had once played alongside Mia—insisted that the color of the medal didn't give the full story. "They won the silver medal, but their game was golden tonight," Heinrichs said. "I'm incredibly proud of each one and incredibly proud of their achievements."

After a little time to recover from the loss, Mia realized her coach was right and she *should* be proud of what her team had done. As she and her teammates assembled for the medals ceremony, Mia walked around to all of them and gave a little pep talk. "She said, 'Hold your head high and be proud,'" Brandi Chastain remembers. "And we were."

❝I wake up every morning and I'm a soccer player, and that's a pretty cool feeling.**❞**

—MIA HAMM

If Mia was worried that her fans back home would be upset that she and her team had fallen short of gold, she soon discovered how wrong she was. Support for the U.S. women's soccer team was still strong, and the players were again in demand for appearances on TV and in magazines.

But Mia had something else to keep her busy. It was time to start practicing with her new team, the Washington Freedom!

As excited as Mia was to be part of the first American professional women's soccer league, there were some adjustments she had to make. Top players from around the world were coming to the United States to play alongside the Americans in the league. So suddenly Mia and her friends from the national team had to welcome teammates they were used to looking at as rivals. It was especially hard for Mia to think about having players from China and Norway in the league since the two countries had the most intense rivalries with the United States.

Not only was Mia now side by side with players she'd competed against for years, but her new rivals were the women she'd played with on the U.S. national team—women she considered her closest friends, even like sisters.

Suddenly everything was all mixed up. Her enemies were her teammates and her former teammates were now her enemies, on the field at least.

It was tough for a lot of the players to get used to the changes and to learn how to play with a new group of people. In 2001 Mia's team, the Freedom, had one of the roughest seasons of the eight teams and shared the worst record with the Carolina Courage. Both teams had only six wins, with 12 losses and three ties. But Mia was still having fun playing the game she loved, and her numbers showed it. She tied for the top spot on her team in numbers of goals and assists. She also came in fifth in the entire league for number of shots taken, proving she was still as hardworking as ever. Mia was disappointed that her team didn't make it to the play-offs and have a chance at the first Founder's Cup championship, but she couldn't wait to try again the next season.

Meanwhile, Mia was facing a very sad experience in her personal life. Over the years, she and her husband, Christiaan, had tried very hard to make their marriage work, but both of their jobs called for them to spend a lot of time traveling. They finally realized that the long-distance relationship was too difficult and decided to divorce. Mia relied heavily on the support of her family to help her make it through. She also looked to soccer to ease her sadness, as she always had in the past.

Before the 2002 season began, Mia was surprised and touched to receive a very special honor. In December 2001 FIFA awarded its first ever FIFA World Women's Player of the Year award, and the 72 women's national team coaches who voted chose Mia in a landslide. (Her closest competitor received only about half as many votes as Mia did!)

Mia had already experienced so many firsts in women's soccer, but this one was extra special. "I'm extremely honored,

Shortly after Nike named one of its buildings in Oregon the Mia Hamm Building, Mia visited the company. She got separated from her Nike guide at one point and was stopped by a security guard because she didn't have a visitor's badge. When the guard asked for a photo ID, Mia awkwardly pointed to the giant mural of herself on the wall next to them and asked, "Will that do?"

first of all, because of the company I'm in," she said in her acceptance speech. "And I'm grateful to FIFA for taking the step and creating an award for this side of the game. It shows their commitment to keep improving women's soccer and investing in it."

As always, Mia cared more about what the trophy meant for the sport she loved than what it said about her as a player. But that didn't mean she didn't want to keep playing the best game she could—she was determined to help the Washington Freedom to a better record in 2002.

Unfortunately a knee injury kept Mia sidelined for the first chunk of the season. She had surgery in February and wasn't able to come back onto the field until June. But in her first game back, against the Boston Breakers, she let loose all the energy she'd been keeping inside, scoring the winning goal for her

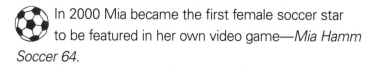

In 2000 Mia became the first female soccer star to be featured in her own video game—*Mia Hamm Soccer 64.*

team. It was just the spark the Freedom needed. They had been on a losing streak until that game, and it was their first victory in over a month. Even after a long career and a recent major injury, Mia proved she still had what it took to be a leader—and she sure knew how to put the ball in that net!

The Freedom took off from there, racking up wins. By the end of the regular season they'd turned themselves around completely from the year before. Now they were in a three-way tie for second place in the league. Meanwhile the team that had tied the Freedom for last place in 2001, the Carolina Courage, had the top spot this year. Both teams were hungry to redeem themselves and go for that second Founder's Cup.

On August 17 the Washington Freedom faced off against the Philadelphia Charge in the play-off game that would decide who went to the championship. Washington had been red-hot ever since Mia returned, and they came into the game on an undefeated streak of seven wins and two ties.

Since Mia was still not at full strength, she sat out the first half. Neither team scored while Mia was on the bench, but the commentator reminded everyone that "the weapon's coming off the bench at halftime." Even if Mia didn't score one of her incredible goals, just her presence on the field could give the Freedom the edge they needed.

The prediction proved right. In the eightieth minute of the game Mia's teammate Monica Gerardo scored for Washington, giving them a 1–0 victory. The Washington Freedom were going to the championship!

The Carolina Courage also won their play-off game, giving fans the matchup they wanted. The two teams with the worst 2001 records would now go head-to-head to show who had come back better this year.

Founder's Cup II was held the week after the play-offs, on Saturday, August 24. Mia was totally hyped to play in her first championship game of the WUSA league, even though she again had to wait to come onto the field until the second half. She watched with white knuckles as her teammates fought to control the game but fell behind to Carolina, 3–1.

"The Freedom still have the trump card, Mia Hamm," the announcer warned, and Mia took it to heart. She knew her teammates were counting on her to come through for them, and no way would she let them down. In the sixty-third minute Mia took a pass from her teammate Abby Wambach, the star rookie of the team, and rushed the goal.

Jaws dropped as Mia easily dodged her defender and went in for the kill, shooting an incredible goal that no goalkeeper could have stopped. Now the score was 3–2, and the Freedom just needed an equalizer to keep the Courage from the win.

To Mia's disappointment, it never happened. Even though everyone agreed that Mia's goal had been the most dazzling of the championship, it hadn't been enough to give her team the trophy, and the Courage became the 2002 WUSA champs.

Playing in the game was still a thrill for Mia and a nice way to end a short—but sweet—season. Since coming back from her injury, Mia had led the league with one goal scored for every 63 minutes of playing time, notching a total of eight goals. She was on fire and feeling great about her game. Whatever challenge was up next, Mia was ready!

❝*I know when Mia gets [out on the field], she poses such a threat for an opponent that it gives us a breather, a lot less responsibility.*❞
—WASHINGTON FREEDOM TEAMMATE ABBY WAMBACH

Epilogue

"The Best Women's Soccer Player Ever"

Even though the 2002 WUSA season ended with the Founder's Cup championship, the league's All-Star game was held a month later, on September 21, 2002. Mia turned in two assists to help the South crush the North, 6–1. Many of her teammates from the national squad and her days at UNC had already retired from soccer, but Mia was still out there, playing hard and racking up points.

The All-Star game victory felt good, and Mia was already getting excited about the Washington Freedom's 2003 season. There was also the 2003 World Cup to think about and the next summer Olympics in 2004. Because there was no way the Americans weren't going to fight with everything they had to reclaim their Olympic gold medal!

Sometimes it's hard for her to believe she's really come as far as she has. "I had no idea I would ever be where I am today," Mia shares, "that people would ask me for my autograph and chant my name, that I would do TV commercials and actually get paid for kicking a ball. I started playing soccer because I enjoyed it."

That hasn't changed, but Mia knows she can't play soccer forever. Even the player who's been called the best ever in women's soccer has to retire someday. But when she does, she'll know she played a huge part in making the sport what it is today, something almost as important to her as just playing the game she loves. Mia can't wait to see what the next generation of women's soccer players can do, and she and her teammates have done everything they can to make it possible for little girls to see their own dreams of playing soccer come true.

In 2000 Mia—along with the other members of the U.S. national team—threatened to stop playing unless the U.S. Soccer Federation gave them salaries equal to what the members of the men's team were receiving. Their efforts worked, and now both teams get equal pay. "This is something we all believed in," Mia said at the time. "Some of us might be finished next year, the year after that, so this contract will outlive us."

In Mia's mind, that's what matters most about all the incredible things she's accomplished, all the championship titles and personal records—the fact that what she's done will inspire someone else to go out there and do it all over again!

CAREER STATS

KEY: GP/GS: games played/games started, **G:** goals, **A:** assists, **Pts:** points (*two points are given for each goal; one point is given for each assist*)

National Team

Year	Record	GP/GS	G	A	Pts
1987	4–2–1	7/4	0	0	0
1988	3–3–2	8/7	0	0	0
1989	0–0–1	1/0	0	0	0
1990	5–0–0	5/1	4	1	9
1991	21–6–1	28/24	10	4	24
1992	0–2–0	2/2	1	0	2
1993	12–4–0	16/16	10	4	24
1994	8–1–0	9/9	10	5	25
1995	17–2–2	21/20	19	18	56
1996	21–1–1	23/23	9	18	36
1997	14–2–0	16/16	18	6	42
1998	18–1–2	21/21	20	20	60
1999	22–2–2	26/26	13	16	42
2000	20–5–8	33/29	13	14	40
Total	165–30–20	216/198	127	106	360

World Cup

Year	Record	GP/GS	G	A	Pts
1991	6–0–0	6/5	2	0	4
1995	4–1–1	6/6	2	5	9
1999	5–0–1	6/6	2	2	6
Total	15–1–2	18/17	6	7	19

Olympics

Year	Record	GP/GS	G	A	Pts
1996	4–0–0	4/4	1	2	4
2000	3–1–1	5/5	2	2	6
Total	7–1–1	9/9	3	4	10

College

Year	School	G	A	Pts
1989	Univ. of North Carolina	21	-	-
1990	Univ. of North Carolina	24	-	-
1992	Univ. of North Carolina	32	33	97
1993	Univ. of North Carolina	26	16	68
	Total	103	49	165

2002 POSTSEASON WASHINGTON FREEDOM						
Team	GP	GS	Min	G	A	Pts
WAS	2	0	90	1	0	2
2002 REGULAR SEASON WASHINGTON FREEDOM						
Team	GP	GS	Min	G	A	Pts
WAS	11	1	506	8	6	22
2001 REGULAR SEASON WASHINGTON FREEDOM						
Team	GP	GS	Min	G	A	Pts
WAS	19	19	1710	6	3	15

AWARDS/HONORS

ACC all-time leading scorer in goals, assists, and points

ACC Player of the Year, 1990, 1992, 1993

FIFA World Women's Player of the Year, 2001

Goodwill Games gold medalist, 1998

Honda Broderick Cup (Most Outstanding Female Athlete
in all college sports), 1993–94

Mary Garber Award (ACC Female Athlete of the Year), 1993,
1994

National Player of the Year, 1992, 1993

NCAA Champion, 1989, 1990, 1992, 1993

Olympic gold medalist, 1996

Olympic silver medalist, 2000

U.S. national team's lead scorer, 1995, 1996, 1997

U.S. Soccer Female Athlete of the Year, 1994, 1995, 1996,
1997, 1998

World Cup gold medalist, 1991, 1999

World's all-time highest scorer

BIBLIOGRAPHY

Christopher, Matt. *On the Field with . . . Mia Hamm.* Boston: Little, Brown and Company, 1998.

Hamm, Mia. *Go for the Goal: A Champion's Guide to Winning in Soccer and Life.* New York: HarperCollins, 2000.

Latimer, Clay. *Mia Hamm.* Mankato, Minn.: Capstone Press, 2001.

Rutledge, Rachel. *Mia Hamm: Striking Superstar.* Brookfield, Conn.: Millbrook Press, 2000.

Schnakenberg, Robert. *Mia Hamm.* Philadelphia: Chelsea House, 2001.

WEB SITES

www.wusa.com

The official web site of the Women's United Soccer Association, the professional women's soccer league in America, gives statistics on players and teams and also has an archive of news articles about the games.

www.ussoccer.com

This site, run by the U.S. Soccer Federation, is packed with information on every U.S. soccer team, men's and women's, and has many articles on Mia Hamm.

www.fifa.com

For history and current events in international soccer competition, check out this site, home of the world soccer association, FIFA.

INDEX